Reiki Healing

Heal Your Life with Energy Healing, Chakra Healing, Guided Imagery, and Guided Meditation

Sarah Rowland

Copyright © 2017 by Sarah Rowland

All rights reserved. No part of this book may be reproduced or transmitted in any form or by any means, electronic or mechanical, including photocopying, recording or by any information storage and retrieval system without written permission of the publisher, except for the inclusion of brief quotations in a review.

TABLE OF CONTENTS

INTRODUCTION 1

Chapter 1 *Reiki Healing* 3

Chapter 2 *Higher And Divine Self* 13

Chapter 3 *Reiki Meditation* 23

Chapter 4 *Clearing Negative Energy* 28

Chapter 5 *Balanced Chakras* 32

Chapter 6 *Chakra Meditation* 36

Chapter 7 *Mindful Healing* 41

Chapter 8 *Power Of Positive Thoughts* 50

Chapter 9 *Mindfulness Meditation* 59

Chapter 10 *Energy* 65

Conclusion 77

INTRODUCTION

Congratulations on downloading your personal copy of *Reiki Healing*. Thank you for doing so.

Throughout this book, you will learn about Reiki healing and the many things it can do for you.

Chapter One covers what Reiki is, how it came to be, how it can help to improve your life.

Chapter Two talks about how to find, connect, and awaken your higher and divine self.

In Chapter Three you will have your first Reiki meditation techniques. Pay attention to these, so you don't inadvertently hurt yourself.

Chapter Four will cover how to clear out all your energy fields.

Chapter Five teaches you how to balance your chakras.

In Chapter Six you will find some chakra meditations.

In chapter Seven you will find out how to use your mind to help heal yourself and others.

Chapter Eight teaches us how to use positive thoughts to our advantage.

In Chapter Nine you will learn to do some mindfulness meditation to help improve your life.

The last chapter, Chapter Ten will explain how meditation can help raise your positive energy to help you have a more fulfilling life.

There are plenty of books on this subject on the market, thanks again for choosing this one! Every effort was made to ensure it is full of as much useful information as possible. Please enjoy!

Congratulations on downloading your personal copy of *Reiki Healing*. Thank you for doing so.

CHAPTER 1
Reiki Healing

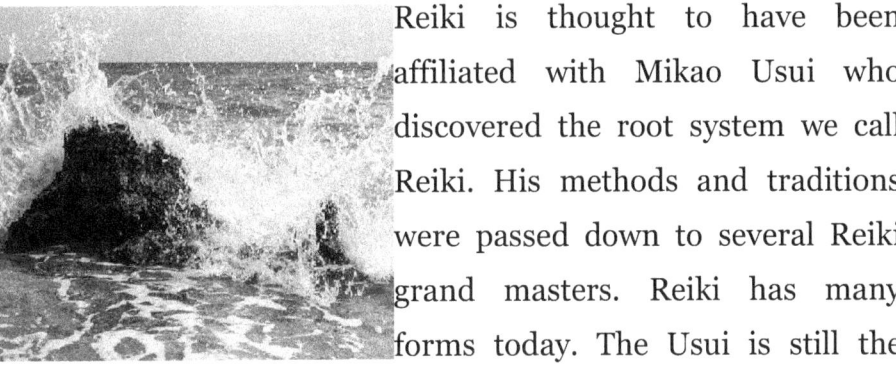

Reiki is thought to have been affiliated with Mikao Usui who discovered the root system we call Reiki. His methods and traditions were passed down to several Reiki grand masters. Reiki has many forms today. The Usui is still the most practiced.

Many years after developing Reiki during a meditation session, Mikao Usui added the Reiki Ideals to the practice. These came from the five principles of the Meiji Emperor whom Mikao Usui admired. These were developed to add balance to Reiki. They are used to help one know that healing the spirit by deciding to improve themselves is necessary for the healing experience. For the healing energies to last, the person needs to realize their responsibility for their own healing and be active in it. The Usui system is more than just using Reiki energy. It needs to include a commitment to improving the system to be complete. These ideas are guidelines for living a kind life and virtues worthy to be practiced for their values.

Reiki healing comes from Japan and is used for relaxation and to reduce stress. It can also promote healing. It could be done by laying on hands and is based on an idea that each of us has a life force energy flowing through us. This is what keeps us alive. If someone's energy is low, they might become sick or begin to feel stressed. If it's high, they will be healthy and feel happy.

Reiki is comprised of two Japanese words: Rei that means Higher Power and Ki that means Life Force Energy. So, the word Reiki could mean "Universally guided life force energy.

Reiki isn't based on any religion or practice. It is spiritual in nature. It doesn't have a dogma, and you don't need to believe in anything to be able to use Reiki. Reiki isn't dependent on belief and will work even if you don't believe in it. Since Reiki come from a Higher Power, many find that using Reiki gets them closer to their Gods. Even though Reiki isn't a religion, it is important to act and live in a way that creates harmony. It isn't massage. It is an active, subtle form of energy that uses spiritually guided life force energy.

Reiki energy flows in every living thing. Practitioners know that everyone can connect to their healing energy and can use it to strengthen their own energy. It gives them the ability to help others. A person's Ki needs to be high and flowing freely. When it is, their mind and body will be in good health. If their energy becomes blocked or weak, it can cause an emotional or physical imbalance.

Reiki is a natural method of self-improvement and spiritual healing that is safe and simple, and anyone can use. It is useful in helping every malady and illness. It works with other therapeutic and medical techniques to help with recovery and side effects.

It is a simple technique to learn. Reiki isn't taught in the ordinary sense, but is transferred during a Reiki class. It is passed during an attunement that is given by the master and lets the student tap into the infinite life force energy to improve a person's health and quality of life.

It is not dependent on a person's spiritual development or intellectual capacity and is available to everyone. It has been taught to thousands of individuals with many different backgrounds and every age.

A session can help relieve stress and tension and can support their bodies to create an environment that can heal on every level like emotional, mental, spiritual, and physical. This will give the feeling of well-being, security, and peace. Many have received incredible results. A session is relaxing and pleasant and done to help a person's wellness. A session can feel like a glowing radiance flowing in and around you.

The practitioner will have a discussion before the session begins. They will tell the client what to expect during their treatment. They ask the client about any issues or problems they are having and ask them what they want from the session. The person receiving Reiki remains clothed. Comfortable, loose clothing is recommended. They will either lay on a couch or massage table or sit in a chair and relax. The session will either be hands on where the practitioner will place their hands lightly in different positions on the body. If a person doesn't want to be touched, they can let the practitioner know before they start. The entire body is treated instead of a particular area. Sessions can take anywhere from 45 minutes to an hour and a half. It just depends on what the client needs.

The session proceeds with the practitioner moving through different hand positions starting at their feet or head. The client might feel tingling or a warming sensation during the session or just incredibly relaxed. They might see colors, or have emotional responses. This indicates that healing is taking place and is allowing harmony to come back into the body. The session should be invigorating, relaxing, and pleasant.

Practitioners aren't trained to diagnose and won't predict any outcome from the treatments. If a person is concerned about a certain symptom, they need to see their doctor.

Reiki is ideal for relaxation and reducing stress. Many will use it for wellness. Reiki doesn't cure illnesses or diseases but might help the body to create an environment to help with healing. Reiki is an excellent complement to traditional medicine and is used in many hospitals and health care facilities.

Reiki is a soothing treatment that could be:

- Comforting if life gets hard: Reiki is relaxing and can be helpful during difficult times. Everyone feels disconnected or overwhelmed at times. Sometimes there is a sense of being isolated spiritually and emotionally. Reiki can bring about feelings of centeredness and peace. We could get the ability to cope with challenges. Reiki is beneficial in short term circumstances but can help people who are dealing with long-term conditions. It can bring a positive outlook, acceptance, and comfort.

- Helpful during pregnancy: Reiki is ideal for pregnant women. Treatments are delightful and relaxing for the mother.

- Help calm children: Children love Reiki. These sessions are shorter than an adult's.

- Reassures animals: Animals respond well to Reiki. They find it soothing and relaxing.

- Gives peace at the end of life: In these cases, Reiki is an excellent comfort. It helps to promote acceptance and peace for the dying and the family members.

One session could be enough, but it needs to be discussed with the practitioner. If you have many spiritual or emotional issues, a series might be more beneficial. If you find that real changes are happening, it is best to continue treatments.

There aren't any known contraindications for Reiki. This non-intrusive treatment can be done in many settings and doesn't need any special equipment.

Reiki is an excellent tool for personal growth and healing. It will create the best results for everyone. It can guide anybody through life. It will assist in creating hidden talents and improve all we do. If personal development and healing are what you want, a Reiki class will be beneficial.

When you begin your self-healing program, take the time to try various techniques. Notice the results of each procedure. If a certain method is moving you to your goal, continue with it. If not, keep trying. By doing this, you will develop a healing system that is right for you. This will improve your results. There are several different ways to use Reiki here are some techniques and ideas that are useful and powerful.

Self-Treatments

Using self-treatments is an essential part of any Reiki program. Take 15 to 30 minutes every day to do a self-treatment. You could do a complete treatment by using every hand position, or you could use scanning to treat just the areas you are guided to. While doing Reiki, your vibrations will go up. When this happens, take the time to contemplate the different activities going on in your life. You will find new attitudes that are developing about certain issues within your life. You will get creative ideas about what to do with them. Keep track of these by writing them down in a notebook.

Personal Healing Alliance

Getting treatments from others is important as well. This helps you keep your energy high. Take it one step more and develop a healing alliance. Find someone that you trust who has a life or health issue they need to heal. Meet once a week to exchange sessions and share what has taken place since the last one. Make an agreement that you will help each other by finding solutions to the issues and become healed. Share everything and keep your meetings confidential. Use your inspiration and creativity that comes to you to solve your problems and reach your goals. Set aside time within the week to send distant Reiki to each other. Call the other one if something comes up. Take these meetings seriously and focus. Never let the meetings become a social event. This powerful process will bring profound, meaningful levels of healing.

Prayers and Affirmations

Reiki can be used to enhance prayers and affirmations. Place your goals on 3 x 5 cards. Use energy and draw Reiki symbols on the card. The recommended symbols are the three Reiki II symbols. Place the card between your hands and give it Reiki. As you do this, repeat your affirmation. You could also say a prayer to give thanks that your goal was achieved or the healing took place. Say this prayer or affirmation over and over. Do this once each day. Carry the card with you and do this when you get a moment within the day.

Go Against the Issue

To accelerate the healing, go against the point and use Reiki to heal any energies or feeling that might arise. Even if you fear do something, do it anyway. Go against this fear. This will stimulate any dormant feelings and cause them to surface where you can use Reiki to release or heal them. It will take courage, but it is incredibly powerful. If you need to, have a friend that knows Reiki to help you. If you fear flying, go ahead and book a flight to any place. Before the trip give yourself Reiki. Focus on any feelings that arise. During the trip give yourself Reiki and concentrate on the feelings. After the flight give yourself Reiki again and deal with any more feelings that arise. If you are just too scared and can't do it, just imagine doing it and direct Reiki to the feelings that come up. By treating the issue in this manner, you will be able to do it in real life at some point. Remember to use common sense and don't do anything that would be extremely dangerous.

Raise Your Vibrations

Whatever raises your vibrations will help to heal you quicker. Do things like eating better, exercising, meditation, getting plenty of sleep and rest, stretching, massage, yoga, social activities, Tai Chi, or any form of entertainment that raises your vibration. As the vibrations go up, it is easier to gain insight into your situation and create solutions. It also allows you to heal better.

Use Other Forms of Healing

Reiki works positively with other healing. With clear intentions and by using Reiki energy, you might be guided to different healing sources. Always look for additional healing methods. Methods like different techniques, diet changes, using herbs, and other homeopathic remedies. These will significantly improve your healing.

Psychological and Medical Care

Numerous doctors and psychologists are open to alternative healing. If you have a medical condition, please get their advice and follow it if your body guides you in that direction. If your condition requires surgery or drugs, get a second opinion before making a final decision. Reiki works in harmony with psychology and medicine, and there might be some therapies they can offer. You need to consider them when you are developing your healing program.

These are just a few ways that you can use Reiki to create a personal healing program. Your clear intentions and inner guidance will enable you to find some that aren't mentioned here. If you are after the greatest benefit, you must be fully engaged in the process. The challenges that we face have the lessons that we need to learn. Don't move away from them. Don't try to solve them halfway. You need to embrace them fully. Accomplishing a personal goal will bring more than just the results you wanted. It will bring a certain knowledge that we can change and create the life we want. When we take a look at our lives, it isn't what we know that is important, or what we do, but what we eventually become.

CHAPTER 2
Higher And Divine Self

Our minds process about forty bits of information every second. The subconscious is more powerful. The subconscious stores the past but lives in the present. This replays within your mind all the events in your past. The ego doesn't trust anyone, always expects the worst, will never forget, will not forgive, rants, blames, defends, judges, justifies, and whines.

The higher self has the ability to get into your energy field. You can engage your higher self by sending gratitude out of the heart into this entry point.

The first step to being able to connect to your higher self is to quiet the ego. The ego is your lower self that lives in your subconscious. By clearing out the energies that we no longer need out of our subconscious, we can connect to our higher self and reunite with the Higher Power.

The higher self is what connects us to the spiritual realm. It is eternal and wise. It awakens our consciousness. It keeps in touch with the Higher Power because it is part of it. By gaining knowledge of our higher self and its wisdom is the primary goal of the spirit.

Everyone can connect to the Higher Power. The higher self can transcend all the understanding in our minds. Geniuses and teachers all possess this power. This is where magic and miracles live.

Here are some ways to connect to it:

Belief and Expectation: You have to believe that you have a higher self to talk to. You have to believe that every day you communicate with it will improve as you focus on inner growth. Without these necessities, you will have a hard time achieving anything. These are necessary for internal growth. Make a goal to contact your higher self, look at it every day, and keep this purpose until you have success.

Change Your World View

The materialist world that we are raised in neglects the Higher Power. To create a close connection to the spiritual realm, you have to your entire being in agreement with your goal. You have to set some rules for how to play the game to reach your primary goals. To get in touch with your higher self is precisely the same. Look for writings and teachers that will help you expand your understanding of the universe as part of the conscious mind.

Solitude

Take some time to be alone. It will need to be a quiet place. Just sit and don't

expect anything. Do nothing. This will feel strange or possibly uncomfortable but stick with it. Take time to hear the inner voice. It will happen during this quiet time or sometime within your day. Something will happen, someone might tell you what you need to hear, or might give you an insight. Every genius throughout history has found time for solitude. You need to as well.

Meditation

You can learn to discipline the internal chaos and quiet the mind with meditation. You will make a clean vessel that your higher self will fill. An excellent meditation training is following your breath. It is relatively easy as you concentrate on a candle flame. You could also visualize a gold ball in your solar plexus that will completely fill your body with energy and healing. There are many different meditations you could use.

Journal

Keep your emotions, insights, feelings, dreams in a journal. This will put you closer to your inner intuition. You can ask it questions and record any answers you get. If you can do this expecting something, you will receive answers.

Inner Dialogue

Have talks with your higher self. Stay in contact with your higher self for 40 days. Tell it that you know it's there and you will pay attention to it. Ask it to guide you and speak to you. This might be a one-way dialogue at first. Keep in mind that you haven't been in touch with it for a very long time. It is going to take time to get everything cleared out. Talk to it just like you are talking to an old friend. Share your hopes. Ask questions. Just talk. Just remember to listen for answers. They will come to you.

Life Lessons

Life is a mystery. Believe that your life was constructed to teach you what you have to know. Approach life as if it was created to do good for you. If something happens whether bad or good, ask yourself what you have learned. Toxic people and situation are there to challenge you. If you can learn to view life as a drama where you are the main character, your higher self will become evident in your life. Write your findings in a journal.

Your divine self is your inner life force. This is your motivation for living. The divine self gives you power and causes you to wonder. It is the light of your core that chose to be embodied at one point in your life.

The divine self if aware at all times. It has been thinking since you were born in every lifetime you've had. The body and physical realm that we are in are what hold the higher self.

You made a decision to be here, and that is why you are here. This energy force provides you with lessons you need to learn. Exchanges have to be made that you can only do as a human.

It may seem like the rules of carnation which are birth and living in the world would keep us from knowing our divine self that lives in our core. This isn't true. You can make a choice for change.

You can acknowledge your divine self and begin to draw it closer to our higher being.

The very first thing you need to do is embrace your divine self.

Shut off your mind as you calm and quiet yourself.

Stop all distractions. No telephones, music, clocks, lawnmowers, children, television, or radios.

Sit where you are comfortable and pick either a candle or mirror.

If you chose a candle, stare into the flame. If you use a mirror, stare at it and look at your whole face. Don't look into your eyes. Don't let the candle's flame make your eyes lose focus.

Keep yourself aware. Stay in your body and remain relaxed. Make sure your eyes stay focused.

The flame is representative of that light that is all life force. All that is alive is powered by light. Everything that is real is perceived by absorbing and reflecting light.

The mirror reflects a self-image that is embraced and avoided.

We try to stay away from it because we compare it to the beauty and perfection that we want to find in the natural world. We don't think about the imperfections of our bodies because it makes us believe that we are unworthy and unlovable.

People don't understand that life is all about imperfections. Conscious energy is perfect and would love to be embodied, so it will experience the joy and sorrow that is reality. It wants to experience the joy and pain that is not perfect and learn how to send unconditional love in spite of these imperfections and sorrows.

This is when you can learn real lessons and get closer to being one with the All. The All is the Creator. The Creator isn't male or female but just is. All is presented just like everything else is; it comes from the Creator. This means that light, awareness, and everyone is always present. Everybody are siblings within the Light Family.

One thing that we miss is that people and things that we assume are perfect have been changed to look perfect and are not natural. Natural Perfection is a lie.

One other reason that we embrace self is ego. Everyone knows we all have bodies. Our bodies have shapes, a mouth, a nose, a face, and eyes. We believe this as truth because we can see and feel it.

When we look in a mirror, we just see a physical thing. Something made up of matter. We might be matter. We do decay and die, but there is more. We feel. We feel love and anger. We cry, make objects with our hands, celebrate religions, reproduce, stay awake and think, and we make choices.

Is that all we are matter? Are we not more like a spirit or a personality that has become embodied?

Personality and thoughts are just a function. They might be powered by a physical function, but it is a bridge between your spirit and body. The brain tries to convert the spirit, but we need this spirit to fuel our lives. If our engines become clogged, we need to look for a neglected spirit for find the reason.

Start looking at your reflection as not just something that is flesh and bone but as a spiritual being that lives in your body. You will then be able to develop a connection to things that are beyond our physical realm.

Stop and just look at your reflection. Notice the light and life that glows and surrounds it.

Do this with a candle or mirror, embrace the creation, the light of life, and your connection to it. Say this affirmation, "I believe in myself. I know it because I can feel it within me. I see it in my life."

Continue to say this and don't be mindless. Repeat it as you feel its truth take hold of your heart. Notice the divine energy and its connection to the universe and the buzz of the creation on the skin.

Repeat this or change it to suit you. Think about your divine self and try to make contact with it.

Stay open to the divine self and keep your heart open so you can communicate with the higher being and see what happens in your life.

Try to do this during a new moon. Continue to do this as long as you need to so you can grow your relationship with your higher being.

At the mystical heart of all religions is a higher being. Understanding this higher being is the most important thing anyone can possess.

Your higher self is surrounded by seven spheres that are your body. These spheres contain your good works. You can look at this as your cosmic bank account.

Your body has spheres of cosmic consciousness that include seven planes of heaven and seven spheres of awareness that correspond with the seven days of creation, the seven Archangels, the seven Elohim, and the seven colors of the rainbow that comes from the white light that is the Father.

Your higher self is part of you right now. It can never be removed. It isn't separate from you in time or space. What separates you from your higher self is your consciousness, your limitations, and the vibrations that you have gotten from all your lives.

Between the light above and the soul below is your higher self. The higher self is part of you that translates an imperfect soul into perfection. It is a part of you that is real and will stand with you in the presence of your God.

This higher self helps you come through all your evolutions and experience in time and space.

Whatever your religion, you can think of this higher self as a guardian angel, a voice of conscience, your inner guru, or your closest friend.

Everyone is destined to be one with their higher self. It doesn't matter if we call it Christ, Buddha, Tao, or Atman.

Your soul evolves on a spiritual path in time and space. It is a part of the mortal you, but it can be immortal.

Your soul's evolution is ascended to the light, complete your mission, balance your karma, and grow your self-mastery.

Your incarnations will end when you become your real self so you can return to your real home. If you pay attention to your spiritual path, the figures that are separate because of limited consciousness will eventually become one.

CHAPTER 3
Reiki Meditation

Silence is hard to find. This noisy world deprives us of subtle and simple experiences. There is an ancient Japanese practice that can let you feel the universe's energy right in your body. This method is Reiki meditation.

Reiki Meditation is a process where you will experience silence and a quiet mind. This meditative energy is loving and healing. In includes mantras and symbols to help your experience.

10 Minute Reiki Meditation

Lay or sit down comfortably on a mat. Keep your back straight. Stay relaxed, composed, and calm. Breathe deeply. Imagine that you are inhaling the goodness and happiness that you want. Now exhale all the negative emotions like anxiety, fear, and depression. Imagine them leaving your body. Do this a few times and think about how in tune your mind and body are. Just relax.

There are seven different chakras in the body. They go from the bottom of your spine to the top of your head. These are energy centers for the body. Put your hand in front of each chakra and hold it for a few minutes. This all depends on what your body needs. If your body asks for it to stay longer, leave it there. Move it if the body has enough. Feeling with the hands is the best way to listen and connect to your body. As you tune in with your hands, imagine the universe's life force is entering your body through the hands. Your chakras are the passageway. Feel your body vibrate with the energy flow. Go into deep relaxation and rejuvenation.

Put your palms together at the top of your head. Hold your hands there and listen to your body. Pay attention. Continue to do this and breathe slowly and deeply. Remove all the negative and bring all the positives into you. Relax.

Put your hands on your forehead. Now move them to the back of your head. Move down to the throat and put on hand on the throat and the other at the back of the neck. Hold this for a time and relax.

Continue down and put your hands on the back of your shoulders. Your fingers should be facing downward. Your touch needs to be gentle. Hold your hands still until the body is ready for it to be moved.

Put your hands on your chest covering your heart. Remember to hold until the body tells you to move.

Move on to the rib area, then the stomach and lower abdomen. Keeping your touch gentle and moving when the body is ready.

When you are done with the head and torso, move to the hips and put your hands on both your hips. Moving only when the body tells you to. Feel the energy flowing through the body. Enjoy the sensations.

Move on to your knees and feet. For your feet, place the hands either on bottom or top whichever is more comfortable. Move your hands when your body is ready. Enjoy the experience.

Finally, place your hands in the prayer position and put them in front of your chest. Sit with the spine straight and the body taut. Breathe normally. Feel the energy coursing through your body. Continue this for another three to five minutes or as long as you feel the need. This process is done when you feel energized and ignited.

Five-minute Body Scan

Begin with the eyes close and examine any sensations that come into the body. Be aware and investigate any place that holds tension and is blocking energy. Let yourself turn inward and work from your toes up to the crown of your head. Stay aware of the different parts of the body and let go of any feelings that come up. Experience them without trying to change them.

25-minute Chi Kung Shamanic Journey

Think about yourself as being very tiny and in your head where your pineal gland is. You are a higher version of yourself. You are glowing bright white.

Feel yourself moving down your spine. Down through the body toward a spot just below the navel. You should be able to sense it. There is a tiny bit of room. Now enter it.

In this room, you find yourself in white robes. A red spinning field is developing under your feet. It looks like fire, but it isn't burning you. It begins to spin faster and faster.

As the field spins, the momentum lifts you. Slowly, while suspended above this field, you feel yourself going back up your body and then out of the crown chakra.

Keep rising until you see your physical body below you and the place where you are sitting. Go until you see trees, houses, and cars as tiny dots. Large geological features become visible. You are so high now that you can see the curvature of the Earth. You keep rising until the Earth is only a dot below you. Move past the planets and Solar System and go beyond, always with the red field spinning beneath you.

You are aware that you are heading to a Star that is your central core. It might be in this Universe maybe another one. It could lie in a timeless space beyond all universes. Your Inner Being knows how to get you there. Feel yourself moving through All That Is until you get to this Star.

You are hovering in space, standing on your spinning disk, and you hear the Star speaking to you. You might hear actual words, maybe not. Information might just get downloaded for later use when you need it. You might see images, or receive a sense of love and oneness with the very core of your being. You can stay with your star as long as you want to.

When you are ready to return, you can move quicker than when you came out. Go through all the steps and return through the universe to Earth, through the atmosphere back into your crown chakra. Continue into the room and cast off your robes. Come back up the spine. Begin to come more into yourself while still meditating.

If you called for your guides to help, thank them now. When you are ready, open your eyes.

CHAPTER 4
Clearing Negative Energy

Have you ever had a sudden onset of tiredness for no reason? You might have caught onto someone's bad energetic field. The trauma from your ancestors, other people's emotions, or negative Feng shui in a room can create havoc in an energy field. This can cause problems like depression, fatigue, or chronic illnesses.

Everything has an energy field. This energy must be maintained properly. Just as our bodies have to get rid of waste, the energy fields of every living thing need to eliminate some toxins. The toxins aren't visible, and can't be measured, but they have the ability to affect us.

The cleanliness of our energy fields is usually overlooked, even in alternative or holistic practices. This is incredibly easy to do. You don't need strength. You don't need to send or gather energy. You don't even have to manipulate energy. You just work with information like working with a computer program.

Here are some ways you can clear your energy fields, so you will no longer suffer any ill effects of having a clogged energy field. These are helpful for empaths.

- Cut ties

This one doesn't clear out your energy field, but it will help to keep them from getting clogged. If you are an empath, you are good at creating relationships, and people are drawn to you. They take your energy but don't give you any in return.

Connections with people whether past or present like family members, friends, or lovers can stay with you long after the relationship is over. Now is when you need to cut ties. You must make a choice to do this. No one can do this for you.

To cut these ties, you just have to picture this person and picture the cords being cut. Bless them and let them go.

- Clear the negative thoughts out of your aura

The mental body is always interacting with other mental bodies. We can pick up negative thoughts that others are thinking. Negative thoughts can be fed for several years if they are connected to any bad experience.

These thought-forms vibrate through you that will cause a cascade reaction in every level of your energy: emotional, etheric, physical, mental, and spiritual. These energies can cause you to attract situations, people, and experiences in your life that will have the same vibrational alignment. If you have negative energy, you will only attract negative experiences.

To clear this, look at your life and figure out if you have been attracting anything you don't like. You have been vibrating in alignment with these things. This is sometimes referred to as the law of attraction.

Begin checking your energy field through the day if you have been feeling off, to see if you have picked up some negative thoughts. If you have, then let them go.

To do this, picture a white light cleaning your aura of all debris and anything that hasn't been serving you positively.

- Have a Sacred Space

You can make a sacred space anywhere that you can spend some time by yourself. This needs to be a space where you can express yourself freely. This might be an office, an art room, or a meditation room. The most important thing is that this is your room. You can't share this space. It is okay if a pet or child walks in since that is hard to control. They need to just pass through and not stay. You don't even have to have the space inside.

Be creative, but this place needs to be one that you go to once a day. If you can't create an actual physical space, make on in your mind and take time to go there. It's amazing what your mind can come up with.

- Smudging

You absolutely must do this. It is very effective. This needs to be done on a regular basis especially if you have endured a bad situation. Use a bundle of white sage and smudge your house and yourself regularly.

- Get in Touch with Nature

Take a hike or nature walk if you start to feel overwhelmed. Negative thoughts are found in humans so spending time with nature is a wonderful way to get yourself recharged. Connect with water, flowers, animals, and the landscape. The beautiful thing about this is it is free.

- Sea Salt Bath

Sea salt does an excellent job at cleaning your energy. Sea salt draws out negative energy. Take a hot bath with sea salt if you start to feel overwhelmed. If you don't have sea salt, you can use regular salt, Epsom salt, Himalayan salt, or whatever you have on hand.

Add some essential oils to your bath if you would like. Be sure to test them to make sure you aren't allergic to any. Eucalyptus, Citronella, and rosemary at the best ones to use.

CHAPTER 5
Balanced Chakras

When someone talks about balancing their chakras, they could be referring to different meanings or techniques. One definition of chakra balancing is the process where the chakra's energy is brought into a harmonious and functioning state.

Balancing the chakras is just one part of the picture: Each chakra is a part of a system that works as a whole. Each chakra connects with the others, and they interact energetically. When balancing the chakras, we must think about each chakra, their neighbor, and the energy they hold as a whole unit.

Balancing the chakras falls into three categories. The ones that are centered on physical activity, a meditative practice, and passing energy from another.

Some practices that you can use to balance the chakras are:

- Alternative or holistic medicine.
- Breathing practices.
- Exercises that connect the mind and body like yoga.
- Self-inquiry and meditation.
- Energy or hand on healing.

There are practices that help to restore balance to the chakras for well-being.

The common ones are:

- Pranic healing
- Craniosacral therapy
- Reiki

Using healing stones or crystals can support chakra balancing activities.

Why would you need to balance your chakras? To help support the flow that sustains your energy level. We are subjected to many activities that are demanding and stressful that can cause fluctuations in the energy. Some people might feel nourishing, fulfilling, or draining. Past experiences and events can influence how we feel in the world and how we manage our daily energy.

Stress that is put on us by life's demands might cause fluctuations and interruptions in our energy flow and causes our chakras to be out of balance. Chakra imbalances can cause:

- How the energy flows through the chakras.
- The energy to be blocked.
- The energy flow to increase excessively and doesn't get regulated.
- The chakra's energetic field is displaced.

Balancing regulates energy when it is too much, establishes a consistent flow if there isn't enough, and aligns if there is a displacement.

The seven energy centers that go through the body are the chakras. Each one is situated in a different location so they can correlate with different ailments. Each energy center houses our mental and emotional strengths. If we have a physical problem, it can cause a weakness in our emotional behavior. If we can get rid of bad energy, it can help any malfunction, stiffness, or tightness in an area.

Clearing energy can balance our state of mind. Balancing the chakras is a two-way street. If we have certain emotions or fears that we hold onto, we will have some physical restrictions.

Using affirmations is highly effective when balancing the chakras. Thoughts can create your reality. When you begin using chakra balancing affirmations regularly, you can achieve amazing results.

The word chakra translates to a spinning wheel. Every chakra corresponds to a certain color-coded vibration in the universe that influences our spiritual, emotional, and physical well-being. If the chakras are aligned right with the universal energy, every aspect of our lives will be harmonious and joyful. We can have perfect health. Our passion and love for life will become renewed.

When you use affirmations, sit or lie in a comfortable and quiet place where you can focus. When speaking an affirmation, visualize a spinning wheel going in a clockwise direction in the color that corresponds to each chakra.

CHAPTER 6
Chakra Meditation

We have covered how to balance your chakras to improve your life. This chapter will cover a meditation that can help you balance them. This is just one meditation that will cover the complete chakra system. You need to make sure you have enough time to completely do this meditation. This will take about 25 minutes. This is not ideal for your very first meditation.

It is very important that you have experience with basic and mindfulness meditation before you start this chakra meditation. Let's begin.

Sit in a position where you are comfortable. This can be cross-legged on the floor, or in a chair with your back straight. Close your eyes and lower down into your breathing, relax the stomach and soften the mind.

Be aware of how you feel. How you are supported and connected to the ground underneath you. Allow your weight to sink into the floor, chair, or cushion.

Hear the sounds around you, and allow them to be there. Notice the shade and light and the air that is touching your body.

Sense the sky above you, the horizon stretched out around you, and the earth below you, supporting your weight.

Let your mind let go and empty everything that you don't need to hold onto. Let it leave, flow out, and go away. Allow the body to do the same. Let it release anything it doesn't need to hold onto. Let it leave, flow through you, and away.

Take yourself away from what happened to you today. Bring all the energy to your center and ground yourself in the moment. Notice the area around you. Breathe with the space. Be aware of the rise and fall of each breath. Notice how it comes and goes, its sensation, temperature, and sound.

Breathe down in the area where your body weight rests, below the spine, into the root chakra. Breathe into this area. Let it soften and grow with each breath, bring nourishment and life force energy into it.

Let the root chakra connect into the ground below you, deep within the earth. Bring the color red in, the color of the earth. Allow the root chakra to be bathed in red. Let it ground, embody, and empower you in the present moment. Let your root chakra take everything it wants. Say these words: "I am here." "I have every right to be in this moment, as I am." "The earth will support me."

When you are ready, continue up to your stomach, just below the navel, to your Hara, pleasure, emotional intelligence, creativity, movement, and choice chakra.

Move your breath in the Hara. All this area to gently soften and expand with your breathing. Bring in life force energy and nourishment. Invite in the color orange, the color of the setting sun. Allow the Hara to be bathed in orange: empowering, balancing, and motivating. Let your Hara be fed and say: "I honor all my needs." "I will allow myself this nourishment."

When you are ready, change your focus to the area just below the breastbone to your Solar Plexus, your power chakra.

Breathe into this area. Let the solar plexus expand and gently soften with your breath. Bring in the color yellow, the sun's color. Let your solar plexus be bathed in sunshine: restoring, replenishing, and nurturing. Let the solar plexus take what it needs. Say this: "I am worth my weight in gold." "I am enough." "I am more than enough." "I greatly value myself."

When ready, move up to the center of the chest, the heart, unconditional love, and the self-development chakra.

Slowly breathe into your heart. Let it expand and soften with each breath. Bring in the color green. The color of spring. You can bring in the color rose pink if green doesn't speak to you. Let your heart be bathed with renewal, healing, and nourishment. Let your heart take what it needs and say, "I am nourished with love." "I will give and receive love freely." "I am completely loved."

When you are comfortable and ready, move up to your neck, your throat, personal will, and self-expression chakra.

Allow the throat to expand, soften, and breathe. Bring in the color blue, the color of the sky. Let your breath bring the sky into your throat. Let it free the creativity and self-expression, softening the need to control, opening, and clearing. Let the throat take what it wants. Speak, "I will go with life's flow." "I express myself." "I speak and hear the truth."

When ready, move your focus to your forehead, between your eyebrows, into the third eye, the wisdom and intuition chakra. Let it breathe, expand, and soften gently.

Bring in the color indigo, the night sky's color. Let the third eye be bathed with indigo. With balancing, clarity, soothing, insight, and understanding. Let the third eye take all it wants.

Say: "Everything is unfolding as it should."

In your time, move your focus to the top of your head, your crown, the oneness chakra. Allow your crown chakra to breathe.

Bring in the color violet and bathe your crown chakra in this color. Allow it to restore, harmonize, and balance. Let your crown chakra take what it needs. Say, "I am one with the whole." "I am one with the universe."

When you feel ready, bring yourself back to a whole, back into your normal flow of breath, back to your center. Breathe deeply into the core, and say. "I am perfect as I am." "I am whole."

Allow the word's energy bathe your spirit, mind, emotions, and body. Let your body take what it needs. When you are ready, let yourself become aware of the air touching your body. Notice the sounds near you and far away.

Let the chakras close just a bit. You just need the intention. Be aware of the support from below. Notice how it feels and holds you in loving kindness for the unique, amazing, and beautiful person you are. When you are ready, bring the meditation to a close and slowly open your eyes. Notice how you feel and how your surroundings have changed.

Do not use this meditation as an everyday practice. Use it only when you feel like the chakras need cleaning. You can set a schedule for when to use this meditation. It might be once a month, when the seasons change, or whatever works best for you.

CHAPTER 7
Mindful Healing

A revolution has happened over the past few decades with how we look at the body. What looks like just another anatomical structure, is really a process that is a constant flow of information and energy. At this very moment in time, your body is moving things around, shuffling and exchanging molecules and atoms with everything else in the universe. This is done at a speed faster than you are able to change clothes. The body that you have this very moment is different than the body you had a few minutes ago.

Every cell in your body is constantly communicating with each other, so they are able to fight off diseases and infections, eliminate toxins, digest food, keep your heart beating, and other functions that keep you alive. These processes might seem like you don't have any control over them, but in fact, research has found that nothing holds more power over the body than the mind.

Every time you think, you are using brain chemistry. When you experience any feelings, emotions, or thoughts, you are making neuropeptides. These molecules go through the body and get in touch with receptors, neurons, and cells. The brain gets information, turns the information into chemicals, and tells the whole body that it can either celebrate or trouble is coming. The body is affected as the neuropeptides go through the bloodstream, sharing the effects of what the brain is feeling and thinking.

If a person says their heart is happy, then they have a happy heart. If a person could look inside that heart, they would find that is being affected by the molecules that create happiness and joy such as huge amounts of serotonin and dopamine. If a person is constantly sad, their skin could be looked at, and they would see large amounts of cortisol.

To harness this unlimited power within the mind, you need to expand your self-awareness. If self-awareness is closed, the flow of information and energy throughout the body and mind is hindered. This will cause people to remain in toxic emotions like regret, self-pity, and resentment. Habits like not getting enough exercise or overeating will take hold. The feedback loop that travels between your body and mind will be negative, and stress will grind away at your life, or you will feel it hit instantly.

If self-awareness is open, then the energy can freely flow. You will be more flexible, creative, and balanced. You will be able to see the world and yourself with understanding and compassion. You will become open to new things. You will experience more energy. With this awareness, you will have the power to create a new reality for yourself. A reality that is filled with well-being and health.

There are many different ways that you can expand your awareness that includes mindfulness and meditation. A self-aware approach to your life will include:

- Don't fear the future or regret the past. This will only bring more misery and self-doubt.
- Redefine yourself every day.
- Don't keep secrets. They can cause shadows in the psyche.
- Get emotionally free. Being resilient emotionally is better than being rigid.
- Work through blocks like guilt and shame. The will falsely color your reality.
- Take responsibility for your conscious choices.
- Examine every point of view as if they were your own.
- Never let denial censor incoming data.
- Don't allow the feedback loop to get shut down by judgment, prejudices, or rigid beliefs.
- Remain open to input.
- Stay passionate about your life and experiences.

Let's take a look at how we can house that power to help you heal yourself. A 37-year-old woman from Hungary was diagnosed with breast cancer. She did not want to undergo any conventional treatments. The doctors wanted to remove her breasts. She didn't want to have that done. She felt like the answer was deep inside her. She turned to reflexology and Reiki healing before she

learned about German new medicine. German new medicine showed her that cancer was caused by emotional conflicts. These things did not work for her, and her cancer began to spread. She went to Lourdes looking for a cure.

Let's pause here for a moment. Knowing that the mind can heal you isn't harmless. If these claims are made without evidence, it can create a false hope. If this person wants to totally reject conventional treatments, then they could die.

It isn't surprising that skeptics write off healing thoughts as evil and a threat to humanity. They brand it as a placebo effect or just plain quackery. The truth is these claims don't have any scientific proof either. Even though the mind can't completely heal you, the use of conventional medicine will probably be needed. There is growing evidence that the mind can influence your physical health.

Your state of mind does play a large part with problems like fatigue, depression, nausea, and pain. Burn patients find about a 50 percent better reduction in pain when using virtual reality games instead of traditional painkillers. Placebo medications work with the mind. The mind expects the medicine to do something and that reflex releases dopamine and other chemicals.

If you have trouble believing that your body harnesses this power, look at these examples from medical literature:

- Some veterans that had been plagued with severe osteoarthritis regained pain-free mobility after they had sham or placebo surgery. The surgeon made a small incision on their knees and sewed them back up. They didn't do anything to their knees.
- A woman had suffered from depression was impressed with how well her depression had lifted that she assumed she was in the active drug group. She found out that she was in the placebo group.
- A man was diagnosed with incurable cancer and died soon after; his autopsy showed that he was actually misdiagnosed.

To be able to tap into this power is by mental rehearsal. You do this by picturing the desired outcome in a way that causes your thoughts to be more real than the world around you. If you can combine a clear intention of what you want with positive emotion, gratitude, and joy, you will be able to give your body a taste of what could possibly happen in this present moment.

If you are able to make this visualization real enough, the brain can't distinguish the difference and will make new neurons and make connections until things start to appear just like the event actually took place. In a quantum physics standpoint, all the possibilities do exist in the current moment, you then pick a new future from these possibilities, you will be successful in your use of mental rehearsal to make it feel real, it is possible to observe this new future into reality by changing your DNA.

What this means is that you become someone new because the body and brain can't identify with who you used to be. By doing this, you actually become a placebo. This will work for anyone. You don't have to be a spiritual master or neuroscientist for this to work.

To get you on the right track, here are some ways to get your mind working to help your body:

1. Help your treatments to work by expecting them to work.

This goes back to how effective this placebo effect could be. If someone tells you that a pill can cure your headache, the treatment is likely to be helpful, even though the pill doesn't have any medicinal qualities. If you go to a chiropractor for back pain or a physical therapist for a bad knee, you believe these treatments are going to be helpful for them to actually be effective.

2. Keep a gratitude journal to get better sleep.

If you have insomnia, using a gratitude journal might be able to help. Studies show that gratitude is linked to quality and longer sleep. Before you go to bed, write down three things that you are grateful for. Doing this right before you go to sleep will increase the odds of getter a better night's sleep.

3. Focus on your life's purpose and live longer.

If you feel like you have a purpose in life, then you have a chance of living longer. Research shows that people who believe that their lives have a purpose live a longer and healthier life. This means that if you find a purpose for your life, or you find meaning in volunteering in your community, just do something that matter to you. Give yourself a reason to want to get out of bed every morning

4. Stay optimistic, and your immunity will get a boost.

Plenty of research has shown that people who are optimistic are less likely to get sick. They used to believe that optimistic people just took better care of themselves, but recently they have found that their hopeful outlook is what is boosting their immunity.

If you can look on the bright side of things, you are less likely to get a cold or infection since your immune system can perform at peak efficiency.

5. Meditation slows aging.

Meditation can provide you with a buffer from effects that stress leaves on your body. Meditation can also slow your rate of cellular aging. This means you could stay looking youthful and avoid age-related diseases with meditation. Research has found that if you teach children to meditate, it will give them lifelong benefits. It doesn't matter how old you are; it is never too late to get health benefits from meditation.

6. Imagine yourself working out; you can build muscles.

It would be great if you could become buff by imagining you are lifting weights? This might be possible because research has found that using imagery can help you gain muscle growth without lifting a finger. One study found that people who pictured themselves lifting weights had a 24 percent increase in muscle strength. People who actually lifted weights had better results, but research still showed that mental training worked and did result in change.

7. Laughing can reduce heart disease.

If you want a healthy heart, then think about something that makes you laugh. Laughter can decrease stress hormones and increase your good cholesterol. It can also reduce inflammation in the arteries. The effects of laughter can last up to 24 hours after you laugh.

Your mind could be your worst enemy or your best friend. Begin to train your brain, so it will help your body perform at it very best. Everyone can build their mental strength. With some practice, mental exercises might just be your key to living a happier and longer life.

CHAPTER 8
Power Of Positive Thoughts

The phrase positive thinking sounds wonderful on the surface. Most people would rather have positive thoughts than negative ones. This phrase is a fluffy one that is usually dismissed in the real world. It doesn't carry the same weight as a phrase like hard working or work ethic. These views are changing.

Research and people are telling us that positive thinking isn't just about being happy, or pasting a smile on your face to everyone to see. Positive thoughts add real value to your everyday life and can help build skills that will last longer than a pasted-on smile.

A positive psychology researcher from the University of North Carolina, Barbara Fredrickson has helped to prove the power of positive thoughts on everyday life. Let's look at what she found and what it means for you.

Let's take a look at what negative thoughts can do to your brain. Imagine this.

Pretend you are walking in the woods. A tiger suddenly appears before you on the path. When you see the tiger, your brain automatically creates a negative emotion. For this example, it is fear.

Researchers have known for a long time that negative responses can cause you to act a certain way. Such as if a tiger crosses your path, you are going to run. Nothing else matters in that moment. Your attention is on the tiger, the fear, and how you plan on getting away.

This means that a negative emotion will narrow the focus of your mind and thoughts. At this moment, you could choose to grab a stick, climb a tree, or pick up a leaf. Your brain ignores these options because they aren't relevant when you have a tiger standing in front of you.

This is a wonderful thing to have if you need to save yourself, but in today's world, you don't have to fear walking up on a tiger in the woods. The bad news is, the brain still has a programmed response to negative emotion, and it will shut out the rest of the world and will limit what you see.

One other example is if you are fighting with someone. The anger and emotions you feel might completely consume you, and you won't be able to think about anything else. If you are stressing out about everything you need to get done today, you might find it hard to focus on what you need to do or how to get started because the length of your list has you paralyzed. You might feel bad because you haven't been eating right or exercising. All you can think about is your willpower and thinking that you are lazy. This is causing you to not have any motivation.

With all of these examples, your brain shuts off to the outside world and just focuses on the emotions of stress, anger, and fear, just like with the tiger. The only thing negative emotions do is prevents your brain from seeing other options that might be around you. This is a survival instinct.

So, what do positive thoughts do to the brain?

Fredrickson created an experiment to see if positive emotions impacted the brain. In this experiment, she divided her subjects into five separate groups and showed them different movie clips.

Two groups were shown clips that created positive emotions. One group was shown things that caused tremendous joy. The other group was shown things that created contentment.

The third group was the control group, and they were shown things that caused no significant emotional change.

The last two groups were shown clips that caused negative emotions. One of the last groups saw images that created fear; the other was shown things to cause anger.

Once they had seen the images, all participants were asked to picture themselves in a place that would cause the same emotions to come up and write down what they would do. They were given a sheet of paper that had 20 fill-ins the blank lines that started with "I would like to..."

The participants that were shown images that caused fear and anger were not able to write down as many responses. The participants that were shown images that caused contentment and joy could write down a lot more actions than even the control group.

This means if you feel positive emotions like love, joy, or contentment, you will see more things that you could do in life. The findings showed that positive emotions could broaden your sense of possibilities and open your mind.

More interesting discoveries came later.

Benefits from positive emotions don't end when the emotion ends. You receive the most benefits from these emotions with an ability to build greater skills that you could use later in life.

Children that run outside, swing in tree branches, and play with friends are developing physical, social, and creative skills by moving athletically, playing and communicating with others, and learning how to explore the world. This happens because the emotions of joy and play are prompting the child to build these skills that will be useful to them later in life.

These skills will last them longer than the actual emotions that initiated the learning. Negative emotions have a different effect since building skills for the future are irrelevant to the brain in a moment when you are faced with immediate danger or a threat.

These thoughts and emotions can greatly impact your life. It is important that you learn more about positive thinking.

Don't misunderstand what is meant by positive thinking. This doesn't mean that you turn a blind eye to the bad things in life. Positive thinking means that you approach unpleasant moments positively and productively. You must believe that only the best will happen.

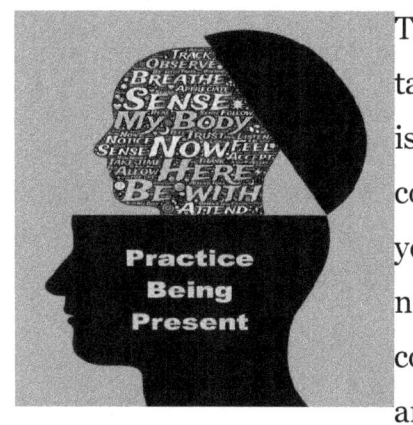

Thinking positively starts with self-talk. If you don't know what this is, it is the stream of unspoken communication that goes through your mind. These thoughts can be negative or positive. Self-talk can come from reason or logic. It can arise from misconceptions because the lack of information that you have about something.

If your self-talk is mostly negative, then your outlook is going to be pessimistic. If your self-talk is positive, then you will be more optimistic.

Researchers continue to explore all the effects that optimism and positive thinking has on health. Here are some of the benefits:

- Better coping skill when facing stress or hardships.
- Improved cardiovascular health and reduced risk of dying from heart disease.
- Improved physical and psychological well-being.
- More resistance to getting a cold.
- Lower stress levels.
- Lower depression levels.
- A longer life.

Negative self-talk comes in one of these forms:

Polarizing

You see things as either only good or only bad. There is no middle ground. You feel like you have to be perfect or you are a failure.

Catastrophizing

Your thoughts will go automatically to the worst-case scenario. Your regular coffee shop gets your order wrong, and you think that the rest of your day will be horrible.

Personalizing

If something goes wrong, or something bad happens, you automatically blame yourself. Here's an example, your friend's night out gets canceled. You automatically think it is because no one wants to be around you, so everyone canceled.

Filtering

You increase the negative parts of a situation and ignore the positive ones. For example, you had a great day at work. You got all your work done faster than normal, and your boss compliments you on the quality of work and how fast you got it done. That evening, you can only think about doing more tasks the next day and totally forget the compliments you received from your boss.

No need to fret, it is easy to change your negative thoughts with positive ones. It will take some time and effort. It is just like creating a new habit. Here are a few ways you can get started:

- Find areas that need to be changed.

If you want to become more optimistic and practice positive thinking, find the places in your life where you are always negative. This might be your commute to work, a relationship, or basically anything. Begin by focusing on just one area.

- Check yourself.

Every now and then check in with yourself during the day and see what you are thinking about. If you see that your thoughts are negative, figure out a way you can turn them positive.

- Learn to love humor.

Give yourself permission to laugh and smile, especially if you are going through a hard time. Find humor in everything that happens throughout the day. If you can learn to laugh at life, you will feel less stressed.

- Start a healthy lifestyle

Start exercising about 30 minutes a few days a week. If you don't have the time to do 30 minutes at one time, break it up into three ten-minutes sets. Exercise creates a positive effect on your mood and can help you reduce stress. Eating a healthy diet can help fuel your body and mind.

- Surround yourself with positive things.

Be sure the people you spend time with will add positive feelings to your life. They need to be supportive and positive. They need to provide you with helpful feedback and advice. If you surround yourself with negative people, it will increase your stress and negativity.

- Practice positive self-talk

Try to follow this rule: Never say things that you wouldn't say to a friend. You need to be encouraging and gentle. If negative thoughts do enter your mind, look at them rationally and say a positive affirmation. Think of things that you are thankful for.

CHAPTER 9
Mindfulness Meditation

Another type of meditation is mindfulness meditation. Mindfulness is bringing your attention to what is happening at this very moment. You develop this ability by practice and meditation.

In Buddhist traditions, they believe that mindfulness will bring you spiritual enlightenment and put an end to your suffering.

Studies have been done on mindfulness, and it has been found to help you live a better and happier life. If you spend your entire life worrying about things that you can't change or haven't happened, you are living life in negative emotions. This will lead to anxiety, depression, and numerous other mental illnesses.

When you begin practicing mindfulness meditation, start with just ten minutes a day for your first sessions. When you are used to the practice, increase the time by five or ten minutes, whatever you think you can do successfully. The goal is to do it for 30 minutes a day. You can do it longer, but it isn't necessary.

The goal of mindfulness is teaching you to live in the moment. You might think that you do already, stop and think about where your mind is right now. When you eat, do you taste your food? Do you appreciate it for what it can do for your body? Probably not. Mindfulness will teach you how to have your mind and body doing exactly the same thing.

The best place to learn this is within the Buddhist tradition. The term mindfulness comes from the Pali word sati and the Sanskrit word Smriti. Smriti means "to bear in mind," "to remember," or "to collect." Sati's meaning is also "to remember."

Now that you know a little bit about mindfulness let's move on to some meditations to help you begin living mindfully.

Three Minute Body and Sound

Begin by noticing your posture in this moment. You might be lying down, standing, or sitting. Be aware of how your body feels in this very moment. Now, take time to see if you can notice any sensations that are present in your body right now.

You might notice lightness or heaviness, weight or pressure. You could even notice warmth, coolness, pulsating, movement, or vibration. You might notice these sensations anywhere in your body. You don't have to do anything but notice them.

Be aware of these things with interest and curiosity. Take a deep breath in. As you breathe in, let your body relax. Don't do anything but be present and aware of your body.

Now let all of the sensations just go. Now turn your focus to the sounds around you. They might be inside or outside of your space. There might be many different sounds. They might be quiet or loud sounds. You need to take notice of the silence between the sounds. Be aware of how the sounds come and go.

The mind wants to concentrate on these sounds. It will begin to come up with a story for the sound. You think you need to react to it: I don't like it. I like this better.

Don't do that, see if you can just listen. Notice it with interest and curiosity. The sounds are just happening.

Focus again on your body; presently standing, lying, or seated. Take note of any sensations. Take another deep breath. Let your body soften. When you are ready, slowly open your eyes.

Nine Minute Loving Meditation

To begin this meditation, let yourself feel relaxed and comfortable where you are. You need to cultivate positive emotions, more importantly, loving kindness. This means you desire someone to be happy, or better yet, yourself to be happy. This isn't dependent on anything, and it isn't conditional. This is just allowing your heart to open to either yourself or someone else. Take a moment and check with yourself to see how you feel right this very moment. Let whatever is there, to just be there.

Let your mind think of something. This might be a person, as soon as you think of them, feel happy. Let someone else come to mind. This might be a relative or friend. It would be best if it is someone whose relationship with you isn't complicated. Once you have them in mind, you should be happy. You might even think of a child.

If you can't think of a person, you could choose a pet. Any animal that you feel love for. Let them come to mind.

Feel like they are standing right in front of you. You should be about to see, feel, and sense them. As you are picturing this, notice how you feel inside. You might feel warmth, or your face might feel warm. You may also begin to smile or have a sense of expansiveness. This is loving kindness.

This is a natural feeling. Everyone can access it at any given moment. When you have your loved one in front of you, begin to wish them well. Wish them to be protected from danger. Wish them safe. Wish them peace and happiness. Wish them strength and health. Wish them well-being and ease. You can wish them these or use your own words.

Be aware of the sense of letting this loving kindness come from you and how you are being touched by this loved one.

While you are doing this, you might have images come into your mind. Notice any light or color. You might even have feelings. The words that you say to your loved one might bring out more feelings. Say whatever is most meaningful to you. Wish them free from anxiety, stress, or fear.

During the time you are sending them these feeling of loving kindness, check yourself and notice how you are feeling. Picture the loved one turning around and is sending those feelings back to you. See if you can receive these feelings from them and take them in.

They are wishing you well. They want you to be happy. This means you. Wish yourself to be at ease and peace. Wish yourself to be protected and safe from any danger. Wish yourself to have well-being and joy.

Let yourself take all this in. If you haven't started to feel loving kindness, or you haven't in any other meditations, it isn't a big deal. This is just to plant seeds. If you begin to feel something other than loving kindness, check that feeling. What are you feeling? You might need to learn something from this feeling.

When you are ready, this is not going to be easy, try to send yourself some loving kindness. You could picture this as a light going down your body from your heart. You just need a sense of it. Say this to yourself: "I wish to be protected and safe from danger. I wish to be strong and healthy. I wish to be peaceful and happy. I wish to accept myself for who I am."

Now, ask yourself, "what will make me happy?" take note of what comes up, offer yourself that. You might wish to have meaningful work, close family, and friends, a joyful life.

Now check again and see how you are feeling. Now think of a person or group of people that you would like to send some loving kindness to. See them sitting or standing in front of you. Sense and feel them.

Wish them to be peaceful and happy. Wish them free of all fear, anxiety, and stress. Worry, grief. Wish them happiness and joy. Well-being.

Let this loving kindness to go outward. Let it spread and touch everyone that you want this feeling to touch. Let it go in every direction. This might be people that you do or do not know. People that you have problems with. People that you love unconditionally. Visualize this feeling touching and expanding. Visualize every animal or person that it touches is filled with loving kindness. Each person is changed.

You can picture that everyone, everywhere is peaceful and happy and at ease. When you are ready, take a deep breath in, and open your eyes.

CHAPTER 10
Energy

Everything in this world is a form of energy. It doesn't matter if you can see it or feel it. You navigate through different kinds of it as you go through your day.

Negative, neutral, or positive, you create energy each moment of each day. Whatever you think, whatever you say, what you do, and don't do all give out corresponding vibrations that go out into the world.

If you can focus your thoughts, actions, and words on making positive energy, your life will get better in ways that you think is impossible. Everyone and everything in your life and on your path, will move to a higher vibrational plane.

Wouldn't it be wonderful to transform into a positive energy beacon that radiates beautiful light wherever you go, in everything you do? You can use your higher vibrational state to make this world a much better place.

Good news, you can. Here are some ways that meditation is the best way to increase positive energy and effectively raises your vibrations to the highest levels possible.

Remember the Truth: "We Are All One" Can Boost Positive Energy

Visualize all of us as simply grains of sand on a beach. Each one is a separate manifestation to a whole.

If you are harboring resentment or holding grudges, negative emotions toward other granules can pollute the entire beach.

Is all the loneliness, depression, and isolation that plagues our society really a big surprise?

So, what is the solution? How can we get to a large mass of higher awareness? That's easy, meditation.

The shift of consciousness that is achieved with meditation can make you aware of the most guarded truth that "we are all one."

Poor, rich, atheist, religious, democrat, republican, white, or black. Humans are more alike than different. We have the same motivations, wants, and needs. These are love, purpose, happiness, and health.

Meditation can help you remember that we are in this together. If the ship goes under, everybody jumps overboard.

When you can begin to see your face in others, a miracle can happen. Everybody becomes your other "you." They are you in another form in a different timeline. It doesn't matter what your current path is, we are all coming back to the source.

Do you really need to be in awe that all of humanity's greatest people meditated?

Let go of your negativity, remember your divine self, and find meditation.

The Law of Attraction Can Create Positive Energy

The law of attraction says that all thoughts and beliefs send vibrations out into the universe. The universe will respond by giving you a set of experiences that will validate your beliefs and thoughts.

We are the creators of life circumstances we find ourselves in because our thoughts can become things.

If your mind is filled with limiting thoughts like, "I will not get the job. I won't get better. I will never find my soul mate". Well, if you continue to think this way, you won't. Your inadequate feelings tell the universe exactly what you want to experience.

This cosmic law carries a powerful and misunderstood paradox: your inadequacies and fears are equal to your confidence and convictions.

This wonderful creative force can't discern between what you want and don't want. They all are put on the same page. What you try to resist will stay. What you believe to be truth, will get conceived.

So, what is the secret to lining up with the law of attraction? All the while trying to remove all the limitations that you imposed that are currently preventing your dreams from becoming a reality. Simple, meditation.

The easiest way to increase your vibrations, create positive energy, and make your intents pure is meditation. Meditation will put the law of attraction right in your hands.

We know that like attracts like, so meditation pulls the rug out from under emotions like regret, fear, shame, despair, and anger while it clears the way for the emotions of hope, love, joy, and gratitude.

The stillness and calmness of your mind that is brought by the meditative shift in your vibrational frequency will make you a magnet for positive experiences. This sets your life on the best possible course.

If you would like to charge up your positive energy, plug into meditation.

Releasing Resistance to Develop Positive Energy

Life is similar to driving down a highway. Do you like driving during rush hour where it takes you ten times longer, wastes your time, and causes all kinds of stress? Or do you like waiting a little later and getting there in the same amount of time without all the stress?

We might not realize it, but many of us live our lives going against the grain. We want to control everything in our lives, and we fail to see what our difficulties are doing to us. We resist our circumstances, and our thoughts turn toxic when everything doesn't go the way we want it.

It just might be possible to make sure we are going in the right direction but to supercharge us on the right path to success, happiness, and perfect health. You can, with meditation.

To quote Bruce Lee: "Empty your mind, be formless, shapeless like water. Now you put water in a cup. It forms to the cup. You put water in a bottle it becomes the bottle. You put it in a teapot it becomes the teapot. Now water can flow, or it can crash".

The amount of mindfulness and the depth of thought that can be achieved with meditation can help you realize that the universe is built on polarity. If there is no bad, there would be no good. Our world is made up of dark and light, yin and yang.

Meditation can help you understand and see that the difficult problems that you face are just steps that will lead to a higher level of being. The darkness within your life will only make your light burn brighter.

Meditation can open your eyes to the higher purpose in your life. This will, in turn, declare a peace treaty in your mind that will unfold the most wonderful things in your life.

Your fresh consciousness can shift your spiritual polarity to help others. You can help to improve the lives of others. By doing this, you will supercharge your positive energy and thus allowing wondrous experiences to fall in your hands.

Clearing Energy Blocks Can Increase Positive Energy

Have you ever wondered why you always get a cold right before you have a job interview? Or how the cold winter months makes you feel like you are just can't get out of bed much less leave your house?

Think about your body as a cobweb that traps all sorts of energy, especially negative. Given time, it can become weighted down with fear, worry, and stress. This can cause your energy field to become clogged.

If you have seen numerous doctors about why you are feeling bad all the time, and they can't give you an answer, it might just be that you have accumulated a lot of negative energy blocks. This is bad news.

How do you get rid of all the energy blocks, while raising your vibrations to a much higher level? You guessed it, meditation.

While you meditate, you will tap into the source field that pervades everything and everyone. With each session, divine energy encircles your auric field. This easily and quickly clears and balances any blocks you might have.

By getting rid of the multiple layers of years of anger, guilt, insecurity, doubt, and fear, meditation lets you start to live the life that you were meant to live.

When you swap negative thoughts for positive ones, you will restore the childlike innocence of always being happy. Meditation can make every day the best day of your life.

Fill up with the universe's energy. Get aligned with the divine. Learn to meditate.

Transcend Fear and Anxiety to Remove Negative Energy

If Batman is positive energy, then the Joker is anxiety.

It is extremely easy to become fearful of things we don't want to experience or feel. We fear humiliation, failure, inadequacy, and inconvenience.

Everybody does it, worry. We worry about the future, and this never solves anything. It does limit your potential. It blocks your flow. It paralyzes your positive emotions. The big picture is that anxiety causes more problems than it will ever solve.

Shifting your consciousness into an extremely high gear as possible.

This gear exists with your awareness in a permanent mental paradise. It starves your mind of lower vibrations and feeds it positive energy.

This gear will open your imagination. It will unearth your potential and awakens your creative powers. It will help you to achieve the future you want instead of the future that you fear.

This can be done with meditation.

The best way to get your consciousness to the highest level possible is meditation. Meditation will put you face to face with all the hypothetical fiction you feed yourself that is all your fears.

Just like you strip the outside of an artichoke to get to the soft heart, meditation will strip all the layers of your mind to the center. It brings the finest tools to completely fix your anxiety.

You receive pure awareness through meditation. It will help you realize when you begin to think bad thoughts. It allows you to snap yourself back to your focused, positive, and calm state of mind.

If you can become the master of being in the present moment, meditation will create a fear free zone that will transform you into a happier, more positive person who has the energy to match.

Here are some meditations that can help you get more energy or clear out your energy fields. These are perfect to do in the mornings so you can have a positive outlook for the entire day.

15 Minute Body Energy

Get into your favorite comfortable position. Either sitting crossed legged or lying down. Close your eyes and focus on your body. Notice your breath and how you are breathing. With your mind's eye notice how your breath is flowing in and out of your body. If your attention begins to wander, bring it back into focus gently with your breathing.

Each time you inhale, you are bringing in life force, vitality, and energy to your body. When you exhale, you are releasing stress, negativity, and fatigue from your body. Let these negative energies drain through your feet and disappear. Breathe in and breathe out. Stay with these deep cleansing inhales and exhales. Take ten more.

With every one of your inhales, you are bringing in energy to the body.

You should begin to feel a subtle new energy vibrating through your body from the bottom of your feet to the top of your head, and then from the top of your head to the bottom of your feet. Be aware of the tingling warmth in each cell. Start to visualize the positive energy that is accumulating through your body, and the energies are shining bright like the sun. Take this glowing energy all the way to the crown on top of your head. Take a deep breath in and then release it slowly. You should begin to feel this warmth of positive energy as it begins to radiate over your neck and face. Feel this new peacefulness and lightness of mind.

Take one more deep breath in and let it out slowly. Notice the positive energy moving across your shoulders and neck, down each arm all the way to your fingertips, and across your heart. Feel the love and warmth in your heart. Let this positive healing energy fill your body with unconditional love.

Take a deep cleansing breath. Notice the healing energy that is moving down your body over the hips and down each leg to the tips of your toes. Be aware of how this energy grounds you to the earth. Feel centered, supported, and grounded. Take one more cleansing breath. Your whole body is filled with positive energy. Let this energy flow through your whole body freely. With each breath, let this energy get stronger. Take three more deep cleansing breaths.

Focus on your breathing and feel how this positive energy is flowing through your body. Notice this new sense of alertness and clarity that is in your mind, the vitality and energy in your body, and the peacefulness and positivity in your soul. Let this awaken your soul. Take a cleansing breath. Rest here with your breath and these feelings for the rest of the meditation. Take them with you through your day.

10 Minute Tranquility Meditation

Get in a comfortable position either sitting or lying and close your eyes. Become aware of your breath. Notice the sensations of your breath as it enters your nose with cool sensations, and then warms as it travels to your lungs.

Fill your lungs with a deep inhale, bring in prana, energy, and vitality, your life force. When you exhale, feel your body releasing all the negativity, stress, and toxins that have accumulated during your day.

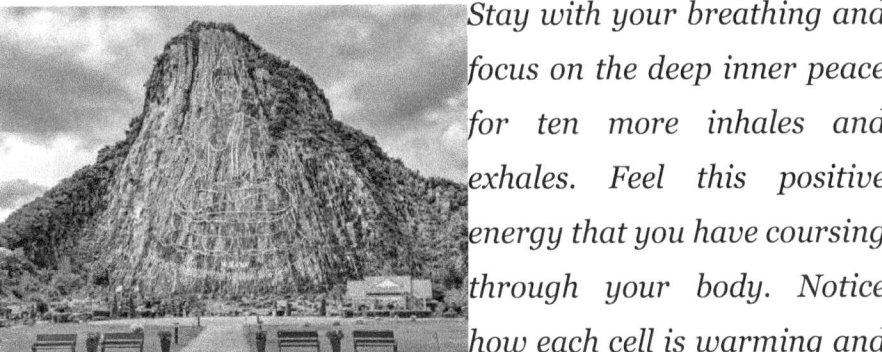

Stay with your breathing and focus on the deep inner peace for ten more inhales and exhales. Feel this positive energy that you have coursing through your body. Notice how each cell is warming and tingling.

Be aware of the energy that is within your environment, in all parts of nature, and in all living things. Take these energies and bring them together so they become as one. Picture these energies shining bright like the sun.

Let this ball of white energy into your crown on the top of your head. Allow this white light to travel down your body. See how it is warming your face and neck, and traveling over your shoulders and down the arms to the fingers. Be aware as it moves across your chest, down your stomach, and over your hips, then spreads down your legs, feet, and toes.

Your body is filled with the warm, divine, white energy and light. Let this healing light to fill each part of your body that needs to be healed. Feel it healing and warmth spreading through your surroundings.

Let this light bring healing and peace to you and to any emotional issues you might have. Change your awareness to and intentions and desires you might currently have. Hold these thoughts about your desires and intentions as you let the energy bring your deepest wishes to life and your intentions into reality.

Feel how you are connected to the light and energy. Remember that it is all one. Stay with this feeling of peacefulness, relaxation, and deepness for the rest of the meditation.

CONCLUSION

Thank you for making it through to the end of this book. I hope it was informative and able to provide you with all of the tools you need to achieve your goals, whatever they may be.

The next step is to start trying some of these techniques in your own life and find out what works best for you.

Lastly, if you enjoyed this book, I ask that you, please take the time to rate it on Amazon. Your honest review would be greatly appreciated. Thank you!